MW01291262

As you journey through these pages, may you be ⤳

Embraced By

LOVE

Shirley Wratten

Shirley Wratten

xulon
PRESS

Copyright © 2015 by Shirley Wratten

Embraced By Love
by Shirley Wratten

Printed in the United States of America.

ISBN 9781498431217

All rights reserved solely by the author. The author guarantees all contents are original and do not infringe upon the legal rights of any other person or work. No part of this book may be reproduced in any form without the permission of the author. The views expressed in this book are not necessarily those of the publisher.

Unless otherwise indicated, Scripture quotations taken from the Amplified Bible (AMP). Copyright © 1954, 1958, 1962, 1964, 1965, 1987 by The Lockman Foundation. Used by permission. All rights reserved.

Scripture quotations taken from the New King James Version (NKJV). Copyright © 1982 by Thomas Nelson, Inc. Used by permission. All rights reserved.

Scripture quotations taken from the English Revised Version (ERV)—*public domain*.

Scripture quotations taken from the New American Standard Bible (NASB). Copyright © 1960, 1962, 1963, 1968, 1971, 1972, 1973, 1975, 1977, 1995 by The Lockman Foundation. Used by permission. All rights reserved.

Scripture quotations taken from the The Holy Bible, New International Version (NIV). Copyright © 1973, 1978, 1984, 2011 by Biblica, Inc.™. Used by permission. All rights reserved.

www.xulonpress.com

ACKNOWLEDGEMENT

In Acknowledgement and gratitude to Almighty God
Father..... Son..... and Holy Spirit
and to all who have helped me come to know Him
and serve Him over these many years.

Thank you to all who have encouraged me to write this
book.....and technologically, patiently helped me
through the process of getting it to print.

"In the day when I called, You answered me; and You
strengthened me with strength (might and inflexibility
to temptation) in my inner self". Psalm 138:3 AMP

"I have declared my ways, my griefs to you, and you
listened to me; teach me your statutes. Make me
understand the way of your precepts; So shall I
meditate on and talk of Your wondrous works."
Psalm 119: 26, 27 AMP

INTRODUCTION

C hatting with you over a cup of coffee would be ideal. Now if you are ever in Virginia Beach, this could happen. But for now, I will let the door of my heart be open to you through my writings and hope that we will have a heart-to-heart hookup that will encourage you and draw you even closer to our loving Heavenly Father.

In desperation years ago, I called out, "God, help me".... just a saying to me,not knowing there really was God Who would answer. Attending Sunday School, church, two years of confirmation classes had still left me clueless and lost. I found religious training does not mean understanding. That can be information for the head only. God is interested in the eighteen inches below the head..... the heart.

In God's timing, I heard the good news of Jesus and invited Him into my life. Awakened in me was such a desire and need to know God, I became like a sponge, thirstily soaking up the word of God and asking Him to help me hide it in my heart. He did. Transformation comes through the Word to a heart that is willing, whatever the cost to the self-life might be. The Holy Spirit has been teaching me, freeing me, and transforming me ever since.... to be continued until I go to be with Him.

Being a self-dependent, strong-willed, don't ask and then you won't be disappointed, self-protective, wounded, unable to trust type of person, I had a lot to learn about God and Who He really is ..... and who I am not. How generously God desires to reveal Himself to us. Only God can restore the years the locust have eaten up and delights to bring healing to our soul and a meaningful personal relationship with Himself. That is why Jesus came ..... to show us the love of the Father.

I have sought and chose God as my companion ..... and not bitterness as my bed partner. Betrayal, rejection, death of a spouse, a difficult marriage ending in divorce after twenty-four years, and the list could go on were included as opportunities to work through. Only God's grace and the touch of the Master's hand of love enabled me to live and keep moving forward when my whole being cried out for relief and resolution.

Maybe you will find yourself struggling with some of the same issues as I. Years ago I told God that if what I experienced would help just one person, the pain would be worth it all. May you be that person.

Love, joy and heart-peace to you. May you sense God's love and touch on your life as He walks with you through this book ..... and always. Come and dine.

Thankful for God's faithfulness, ...
    Shirley

Also known as Mom/Grandma/Great-Grandma and friend
A child of The King of Kings and one whose name is written in the Lamb's Book of Life.

TABLE OF CONTENT

ON A MISSION

LORD,
With your hand in mine
and Your holy design
Our writing will be seen on the pages.

Your words will come flowing
and without my real knowing
Your message will pass through the ages.

Free me, unencumbered
To hear Your still small voice in quiet . . . . . or in thunder
And express what you give me to say.

Holy spirit You will lead me
On the Word You will feed me
For I know I have nothing to say.

A vessel full of cracks
and a great many lacks
You have chosen the least of the pack

So I pray . . . . .

Anoint me from on high
And the words will fly
Piercing the dark with your light.

May our heart be as one
Putting our enemy on the run
Co-laboring with You in Your vineyard.

Pressing on to the goal
Of introducing someone to You

Encouraging and comforting Your children.

I submit all to you
It is because of You
I am thankful for the privileged mission.

LOOKING INWARD

The mirror of God's word
Reflecting back to me
All that is in my heart
That needs to be set free.

Sin that has long held me captive
Robbing me of peace
Needs confession and forgiveness
That I might be released.

Some things long forgotten
Covered over..... pressed down
Seemingly out of sight
Often cause disturbances
In the wee hours of the night.

Tossing and turning
Sleep all askew
Finally asking..... Lord, bring to the surface
What must be worked through.

Replacing old ways of thinking and doing
Reconstruction under way
God is never finished with us
Let Him guide the way.

Humility says,.... "I am willing"
Repentance says,..."I turn around"
Confession says,...."no longer guilty"
Forgiveness says,...."grace abounds"
Love says,...."**I AM** has filled you"
Soul says,...."free at last"
God says,...."I give my beloved life, love, joy, peace, and rest
Purpose and belonging."

REPENTANT HEART

Falling down before You, Lord
Prostrate on the floor
I await Your voice to speak
My heart..... an open door.

You have plowed and plowed my rebel heart
Breaking up the hard and rocky places
Then planted Your seeds of righteousness
Watering them with grace from Your oasis.

Living water from Your well-spring of love
The supply is never ending
Your word..... the foundation of all truth
Inviting me..... Come drink for life unending.

Believe The Way, The Truth and The Life
His life has surely shown me
Repentance granted from above
Newness of life to be made known to me.

We are encouraged to
Humble ourself under God's almighty hand
Submit ourself to Him
Surrender and yield to the Son of God
Then cast all your cares upon Him.

Never surprised by what is in my heart
Always available to draw me near
Exchanging my heart for His
Choosing to be made..... wholly His.

Thank you, Father, for total acceptance
The Author and Finisher of all that is
You sent Your Son..... my heart He has won
For Your purpose You have saved me.

Holy Spirit, lead me...... guide me.
Let me hear You say

Come my child, this is the way
To bring Me glory today.

My Lord, my God
Until that time appointed to bring me home
With joy unspeakable
Before Your throne
With eternal praise upon my lips
All praise and honor is due to You alone.

Even now, declares the Lord, return to Me with all your heart, with fasting and weeping and mourning." Joel 2:12 NIV

"For this is what the high and Lofty One says, He Who lives forever, whose name is Holy:....'I live in a high and lofty place, but also with him who is contrite and lowly in spirit, to revive the spirit of the lowly and to revive the spirit of the contrite'? Isaiah 57:15 NIV

ONE NOVEMBER

I did not know my future
But knew I could trust The One Who held it in His hands
As my husband and my children's father
Went to a war in a foreign land.

I opened my heart completely
Our times were in God's hands
He said He would never leave me and be always with me
On this my life did stand.

After delivering a 9 lb. 6 oz. baby boy
Uninvited..... blood clots arrived at my door
This became a time to reflect on what I "*really*" believed
Should my life not be restored.

I began to understand
The gift of this child was created by God Himself
In His image..... for His glory
Ours for today..... he is God's for eternity
This..... summing up life's story
Our lives..... not our own.

Six weeks after delivery, the year was 1966
In the wee hours of a November morn
Our life would be changed completely
A shock to us must be borne.

Awakened and running
A mortar attack from six miles away
Shrapnel..... straight to my husband's heart
His soul departed this earth that day.

At that moment of departure
Something wonderful must have happened, I believe
Incredible to me..... was a smile upon his face
Forever..... God's kind gift to me
And would speak volumes to all God wanted to see.

That smile forever took away my fear of death
Confident
To be absent from the body..... is to be present with the Lord
This peace and joy on His face was showing
God's word of truth..... and the smile
A major impact was made upon me.

What now?

Five precious children under the age of nine..... and me
No immediate family close by
Learning to trust and lean hard on God
The word of God daily invested and speaking directly to me
My strength in **Him.....** needed to be.

Choosing to walk in God's way of thinking
Brought many challenges and often tears
Peace..... sometimes elusive, without understanding
Humbled..... I would surrender
Laying everything down before Him.

Opening my heart and hands to receive from God
How often I did pray: "Thy kingdom come
Thy will be done on earth as in heaven this day.
As my day is, Your strength I need
Your love and mercy to supply
Our daily bread and needs, O God
Your manna for which I cry."

"Whole..... and wholly mine", Jesus said
"Is a heart transaction for the living
Now is the time
Do not harden your heart
I AM is here..... and here to stay
Each day..... a new beginning."

How often I thought of this provoking question
"What would it profit a man to gain the whole world
Only to lose his soul

And what would a man give in exchange for his soul?"
Heaven or hell . . . . . the goal.

A gifted surgeon with so much potential
Gone in a blink of the eye
I know he would not have given up heaven
For any earthly honor . . . . . or what money could buy.

God so loved the world He gave us His Son
He suffered on the cross for us that we might become one
The resurrection power that lifted Jesus from the grave
Sin and death . . . . . He forever shattered.

His invitation extended . . . . . . Jesus says, "Come"
I have prepared a place for you
To as many as receive God's gift of love
Heavens gate . . . . . opened wide
Eternity . . . . . spent with Him.

Because of the nail prints in Jesus hands
Our lives are always before Him
Nothing can ever separate us from His love
Guaranteed . . . . . a promise He will keep.

Now . . . . . near . . . . . or distant
When it is time for that end of life call
"What have you done with my Son?" God will ask.
A crucial question to be answered by all.

That November 4 morning . . . . . so many years ago
Often seeming like yesterday
Still finds me with God's hand in mine
Thankful . . . . . never abandoned
Always with me . . . . . faithful
A stabilizing blessing all the time . . . . . mine.

Surrounded by so great a cloud of witnesses
Who have gone before
This is written in the hope
That you, too . . . . . have answered God's call.

GOOD NEWS

Jesus proclaimed.....
The Spirit of the Lord God is upon Me
Anointed to be God's word made flesh
Sent to bind up and heal the brokenhearted
And liberty to those physically and spiritually bound
unto death.

To comfort those who mourn..... having no hope
The oil of joy healing wounds
Beauty in exchange for the ashes of life
The garment of praise for a heavy-burdened spirit
His life for mine and for yours.

Love was poured out on the cross of Calvary that day
Forgiveness proclaimed from His lips
"Father, forgive them for they know not what they do"
Each drop of blood that was shed
He felt..... He knew
Given for me and for you.

The way of forgiveness was costly
Our Lord Jesus paid it all
Surrendering His will to the Father
Knowing what was to come
He said, "Father, if there be some other way
Nevertheless, I will"..... and it was done.
ALL was given. It is finished!
Completed by Him.

I heard God's message of salvation
Responding, I received new life through our Savior Who died
His wounded, crushed body given..... I was forgiven
My way to the Father through Him.
His Holy Spirit now living within.

What a joy to be a part of His kingdom plan
Sharing Jesus and all that He means
To see the opening of blind eyes..... now able to see
Eternal life, forever with Him.

CALVARY

The way of forgiveness is costly
Our Lord Jesus paid it all
Surrendering His will to the Father
Knowing full well what was to come
He said "Father, if there be some other way
Nevertheless I will"..... and it was done.

Love was poured out on Calvary that day
Forgiveness proclaimed from His lips
Each drop of blood that was shed
Pain and sorrow..... He fully knew
A request to the Father, "Forgive them
For they know not what they do".

Jesus, our Savior, suffered and died for you and me
His body wounded, bleeding and crushed
Willingly gave Himself you see
For sin that separates us from God..... to set us free
And forgiven..... to belong to Him.

Jesus' request to the Father that came from His lips
Was that we would all be made one with Him
Establishing the way to the Father..... through His Son
Inviting us all to come to Him.

Now to as many as receive Jesus as their Savior
They become a child of God
His resurrected life and love within us to shine
To be reflectors of this amazing grace
A life purchased by His precious blood
A life no longer mine.

When yielded, submitted and surrendered
Belonging to Him..... desiring to do His will
Hope and joy now our companion
No matter what life's circumstance will bring
Nothing to ever separate us from His love

Life eternal . . . . . now and forever
Safe and secure
Looking to heaven . . . . . our final home
With Him.

THE WAIL

The wail deep inside of me
That took Jesus to the cross
Is never really vented
Until I see what **He** gave up for me in what I call
. . . . . my loss.

The depth of love extended
That hung Jesus on that tree
The gift of love intended
To bring Him down to me.

Pure love and grace have saved me
My life . . . . . not my own
My satisfaction to be in You, Lord
Until you call me home.

God of all comfort and encouragement
Once again I have come
You . . . . . never tiring of my call.
Holy Spirit, please fill up the void and holes
The wail inside me ending
When I see Jesus resurrected
And on His loving throne
Interceding . . . . . in a place I will call home.

Thank you.

Sometimes lonely, but never alone . . . . His.
In His keeping, now and forever . . . . His.
Loved always and forever . . . . His.

IN TRAINING

The world is my classroom
God's word, a lamp upon my path
My need an opportunity to find Him
And lay **everything**..... at His feet.

Underneath all of life are His everlasting arms
Holding me up..... never to let me go
How else would I know His sufficiency
Pride, independence and arrogance, needing to be in control
Y*ou*..... need to go.

So if and when I humble myself under His almighty hand
Inviting Him in, spending time to hear
In His loving-kindness
He will always draw me near.

One breath at a time
One step at a time
Is all I have it is true
God is equipping me
As I seek to do His will.

He will show me the path of life
In His Presence..... fulness of joy
I must come with an open hand
To experience His peace, His love and His will.

Lord, put Your arms around me
Hold me ever so close
Grace has now bound me
Your love and joy received when I need it most.

Faithful is He who called me
Never to leave me alone
Teaching me and guiding me
Until He calls me home.

PROFESSING..... POSSESSING

I love you, Lord Jesus
I am glad you are mine
Walking through this minefield called life
With Your hand held tight.

"Who is this coming up from the wilderness
leaning on her Beloved"?
It is I, dear Lord..... it is I..... needing You
Never a circumstance that God is not in control
Amazing possibilities now to be found
Pure love and grace and mercy will abound.

"In You our fathers put their trust; and You delivered them
They cried to You..... and were saved;
They trusted in You..... and were not disappointed"
From birth..... right on to the grave.

O Lord, my Shepherd, I, too, shall not be in want
You..... leading me beside still waters..... restoring my soul
Even though walking through the valley
The shadow of death upon me
I fear no evil for You are with me
Your rod and Your staff to comfort me..... Your goal.

To You, O Lord, I lift up my soul
In YOU I trust, O my God
Teach me Your ways..... show me Your paths
Guide me in Your truth all of my days
You are my hope, my God, my Savior
It is *You* Who makes me whole
Keeping my soul.

The earth is Yours and everything in it
The world..... and all who live in it
I seek *Your* face, in *You* alone I trust
Open up the flood gates
King of glory come in.

Who is this King of glory?
Why the Lord God Almighty ..... He is The King
And now even more amazing
He lives with me ..... within.

Kept by His power ..... enabled by His grace
Peace from the Father with love
He, shedding light onto my pathway of life
Giving sight ..... hope and comfort in my night.

Thank you King of glory for your Son this day.
You Who know my whole life's story
Thank you for giving me new life
Through Jesus, the Christ, Your Son.

Thank you Lord Jesus for dying in my stead
For making me one with the Father and with You
Forever settled in heaven
To be eternally secure ..... now and forever with You.

Thank you for peace
That surpasses all human understanding
Peace not as the world could try to give
But peace, true peace that comes only from *You.*

You O God I would lean on, trust in, adhere to
Seeking to give all my cares, fears and trials to You
Receiving *Your* love that then
Sets me free
To be able to love ..... be filled
And be renewed.

Thank you for what only *You* can do
And for enabling me to know it!

Song of Solomon 8:5; Psalm 22:4; Psalm 23;
Psalm 25;1 "God is love"

SEASONS.... SEASONED.... AND STRETCHED

Are you in a new season of life
Floundering, feeling like you've lost your way
Things unfamiliar..... casting shadows on the path
Like a haze covering a once sunny day?

Without warning, tears can run down the cheek
Like rains against the window splatter
Wondering..... how and why did this transition take place
And do I really matter?

Amazed, perplexed and uninvited
This new "life" has arrived on the scene.
What once was..... is now gone
I lament with a song
The tune, a dissonant reminder.

Reaching out for new light
Though not meant to cause fright
Is a path beyond my comprehension.
Will I yield
Will I fight
Go left or go right
Will I surrender it all to God's hands?

Will eyes of faith truly be mine
Trusting Him *really*..... that all will be fine?
Choices will tell
Am I living by faith or by sight.

This Familiar Hand
Is The One Who has known
My life from the very beginning
Will I yield to His urging, though my mind is surging
Will I surrender seeking His mind to be formed in me
Once again?

I sense God declare: "See ..... I am doing a new thing
In your heart this will ring
Expectation ..... new patterns and ways of thinking
Never alone, My work in you has shown
Delight has been given to The Master."

So as I recall, having learned from the past
With His hand holding mine ..... I know it will be fine
I can at last begin to release apprehension
As I focus in on the vision ..... Jesus has risen
I can be at peace ..... seek ..... and will find.

When temptation arises to hear other voices
Enticing ..... to stray off the path
Holy Spirit enable me
With weapons You gave me
To wield them and drive out the night.

Grace and mercy are constant companions
All peace, encouragement and comfort are from Him too
God as revealed in His word ..... His perfect love
casting out fear
In faith ..... I now draw near.

His love never ending ..... now transcending
To fill me with hope anew
By faith believing, His truth I am receiving
He will guide me through.

So now ..... I will go on living
Fill my heart with thanksgiving
His love for me is all I need know
It will keep me from falling
And keep me from stalling
Pressing on ..... with endurance ..... and go.

A new season ..... a new reason
Another opportunity to know God better
and come to grips with His truths

Quietness and confidence will be my strength
Though stretched to great length
His word tried, tested and true
His plans . . . . . always good
Written that you may be encouraged too!

"See, I am doing a new thing! Now it springs up; do you not perceive it? I am making a way in the desert and streams in the wasteland."
Isaiah 43:19 NIV

"Trust in the Lord with all your heart, and lean not on your own understanding; In all your ways submit to Him, and He will make your paths straight." Proverbs 3:5,6 NIV

PLEASING

I feel scattered, Lord
Going in all directions
Doing a little here, a little there
A need to focus, not obsession.

Read a little
Write a little
Going from one thing to another
Accomplishing "what is important" in my eyes
But then again
Does it truly matter?

Asking you to lead me
My time is in Your hands
It is not my "value" assessment
What was "gained" on how I spent this time
But am I doing Your will, Oh God
Line upon line
Not volume of things done
To check off on a list
But am I pleasing You, Lord
With Your hand in mine.

"Not based upon performance
But, trusting..... believing..... receiving
Exhibiting fruits of contentment..... gratitude
Union and communion
Staying close to Me
Says God.....
That is what means the most to Me.

ACTION

Upheaval in life..... how to make it through
When feeling like a stretched rubber band ready to snap
Nowhere to run..... no other way out
But God..... said He would see us through.

Submit..... yield..... surrender
Trust..... stay hooked to The Vine..... obey
Action words seared into my mind
Powerful words directed by our God, The Almighty,
The Divine.

No..... it is not easy putting these action words into practice
Costly to self..... that wants to be in control
But the peace with God and the peace of God
Ours..... when we yield ourselves to Him body and soul.

Faithful is He Who has called us
Intimacy with us His desire
Perfect love..... casting out fear
Ours..... when to Him we draw near.

He says, "I know the plans I have for you
Not for evil, but for good"
Casting all our cares upon Him..... keeping nothing
in reserve
Believing Him and in Him is what we should.

Stayed upon Jehovah
Our eyes and ears and heart finding Him
No ploy of the enemy will win
But also, no shortcut, no substitute to have victory within.

"The Lord is a stronghold for the oppressed, a stronghold in times of trouble. And those who know Your name put their trust in YOU, for You, O Lord, have not forsaken those who seek you." Psalm 9:9-10

BE STILL AND REST

Running the race of life with patience
Is difficult to achieve
The power to work with a great weight in the heart
A great challenge, indeed!

How easy it is to get caught up
Running around in circles
The secret I found to tame my life down
Is stop . . . . . . look . . . . . and listen.

An inarticulate fellowship
Sweeter than words can express
Union and communion . . . . . full of love
Is my head upon God's chest.

Being still . . . . . and knowing my God
The Spirit interpreting my needs
Interceding for me before the throne
Incense to the Great High Priest.

Because of how Jesus suffered and died
An example to us is shown
Casting all His cares upon the Father
We, too, never walk alone.

Open up the heavens
A vision, O God, open my eyes
Transform all earthly sorrows
As I look into Your eyes.

THIS MORNING

Stationed at the gateway of Your Word this morning, Lord
Giving my faculties full attention to hear and see
A quiet desperation had set in
Then my Heavenly Father said to me.

"Come and sit with Me awhile
I know your need to talk
I will listen to your heart expressed
So you may know your thoughts within.

Once again you have reached an endpoint
Come..... submit it all to me
A load too heavy..... it will break you
Come..... entrust it all to Me.

Deep inside you have carried anger
Lust of all kinds..... gone unfulfilled
Feeling incompleteness in your spirit
That only I, your God, can fill.

I am with you and will keep you
As you look deep inside
Fear not, my love is deeper
No need to try and hide.

Jesus, My Son, given to you
Tells of My love so deep and wide
Resurrection power has lifted you higher
Than Satan's power to rob His bride.

Bearer of My message
Be ready for what I might want to do
Nothing can ever separate us
I give perfect love to you."

Abiding in His presence
Belonging..... safe and secure
Quietly reflecting
I now have His point of view.

A MEETING PLACE

As I dig into the Word of God
Parched..... thirsty from the storm
Battered, bruised from all the strife
My spirit..... shred and torn.

All I know is I must be there
And amidst my tears I see
One Who had died for me
And hung upon that tree.

He is hope..... and He is peace
His life and death my example
He will meet me in my need
His amazing love is ample.

He whispers His secrets to my soul
Giving comfort and encouragement
Wiping away all my tears
His word..... my nourishment.

So when..... not if..... hard times come your way
And you flounder..... not knowing what to do
God's Word is truth and will meet your need
And His Spirit will see you through.

Wait, I say, upon the Lord
Lean hard only upon HIM
Faith grows amid the storms
When God is invited in.

So..... be strong in faith and in the power of HIS might
Step out..... dare to believe Him
Find that underneath are His everlasting arms
Holding you, keeping you near Him.

Love is found and grace abounds
Eyes..... you now see Him
Invest yourself in the Word of God
A time..... the best time..... to hear Him.

"Blessed is the man that trusts in the LORD and whose hope the LORD is. For he shall be like a tree planted by the waters, and that spreads out its roots by the river and shall not fear when the heat comes, but its leaf shall be green; and shall not be anxious in the year of drought, neither shall cease from yielding fruit." Jeremiah 17:7,8 NKJ

LORD, WE NEED TO TALK

I find myself in a very dark place
Concerns, heavy on my heart
Seeing my family in turmoil
Of one kind or another
I feel like the rubber on the tire meeting the road
Worn and tired.

So many hurts . . . . . past and present
Some creating a great divide
One thing for sure we know will not work
is to go away and hide.

Grant us courage to look deep within
Help us work toward a restoration answer.
A willing heart to deal with what is
No excuses is what we need to begin.

We cannot change the past
With hopes and dreams shattered . . . . . and disappointments
Looking us full in the face of what was
Or what was hoped for
Unable to dispel consequences of choices made
. . . . . or received.

So now what, Lord?
We can't start over
But . . . . . can we begin again?

Grace, mercy and peace
Available from your kind and loving heart
Would lead us through transition
New birth be given
As you give us a vision
And a heart that is willing
To get us well on our way.

Walking in the light of today

Leaving the regrets of yesterday
This is the opportunity that lays before us.
Let me hear what you say.

"STOP..... be quiet..... ponder my ways
LET the craziness of thoughts roaring through your mind
be released.
LET my mind and heart be formed in you."

Oh God..... I know You will enable and make us stable
If we come and ask You to help us recognize
And ask You to disable
Sinful patterns of thought and deeds
That turn into hurtful words and/or actions and deeds.

But even If only in our thoughts
Anger turned to rage..... and then to bitterness
Bring death and destruction
To all that it touches
A prison house all of its own.
Action and thoughts without love
Devastation.

Seeking to dull the pain in any other way
Is a trap our choices have shown.
No short cuts will work that is sure
Because without God invited in, we are on our own.

God's cure is to humble ourselves under
His almighty hand..... and in due time
He will lift us up.
Submit. Yield. Surrender.

What will we do with the offer?

A repentant heart which He delights to give when
we ask Him.
A new heart and a new Spirit He will put within us.
Forgiveness both given and received
Healing and restoration

Our need.
ALL was purchased upon that tree
Jesus blood will set us free
Receiving freedom . . . . . union and communion.

Lord, may it be.

CHILDREN

Out of sight
But never out of my heart
Are the children
God has given me.

Now all adults
Some with children and grandchildren of their own
What an amazing sight
Born from a seed that God had planned to be sown.

We are all God's idea
Planned for before He made the heavens and the earth
And at just the right time
He gave us life and birth.

Neve a "mistake"
Each of us particularly designed for His plan
Not by the will of man
But by the Father Himself
Fashioned us with loving likeness
And a joy to populate the land.

If I, being sinful, can give my children good gifts
How much more will our Heavenly Father give to
His children
Perfectly knowing just what to do
To give us fulfillment and draw us back to Himself again, too.

No sorrow or joy goes untouched by His hand
All comfort is from Him, too
Invited to crawl up into His lap
Like most papas and children like to do.

What a wonderful, safe place
In God's loving presence
Total acceptance with real love to receive
I am ready, are you?

REST

Remember and return to Me
All you who labor and are heavy laden
And I shall give you rest
Peace beyond all human understanding
Confidence and strength
Release and rest.

What an invitation
In a land of busy and sometimes harsh living
Wrought with sin and pitfalls
Entangling feet to trip.

How will I respond
What will my answer be
To this powerful call promising rest to me?

"Come to Me, all who labor and are heavy laden, and I
will give you
rest." Matthew 11:28 ESV

"For thus said the Lord God, the Holy One of Israel, 'in returning to Me
and resting in Me you shall be saved; in quietness and in trusting confi-
dence shall be your strength. But you would not.'" Isaiah 30:15 AMP

HELLO!

HELLO! HELLO!

Is anyone there?
It is God calling
Can you hear me now?

I have tried to get through
I have a message for you
Critical . . . . . a life and death situation!

Please . . . . . answer my call
Do not delay at all
Open the line to hear Me.

From My heart to yours
A critical issue to make known
You are just a breath away
From your eternal destination.

Call on Jesus at John 3:16
to confirm your reservation.

A NEW YEAR

A new year is on the way
Filled with hope and expectation
New life experiences awaiting
Not to dread the undertaking.

A tiny seed has been planted
In the prepared soil of our heart
New life to appear
Sometimes watered with a tear
The Master Gardner ..... always near.

The little seed must die to self
So it will not abide alone
But will send out roots and multiply
Bearing much fruit as it is grown.

Only God will know what life will bring
I will desire each day His will
Ask, seek and knock and we will find
Life here and now ..... fulfilled.

To as many as believe Him
And receive His life will see
All things work together for our good
His glory fulfilled within you and me.

No guarantee that life will be easy
In fact the opposite will often be true
But enabled by His almighty arm and great power
His love and presence will see us though.

Thankful in advance
A secret has been found
Yielded and still
Waiting on You ..... expectant
We receive hope and sight
Comfort and encouragement

It **all** comes from You.

Now we see through a glass darkly
One day we will see Jesus face to face
Blessed and assured by His word and grace
Love, mercy and peace offered to the whole human race.

Without a vision the people perish
So please, Father, give us sight
Humbled . . . . . needing you
We submit this year and surrender our life to You.

A new year
Moment by moment
One breath at a time
To honor You and Your plan for our life.
Thank you, Lord, for light . . . . and abundant life.

"Truly, I tell all of you emphatically, unless a grain of wheat falls into the ground and dies, it remains just one grain; it never becomes more but lives by itself alone. But if it dies, it produces many others and yields a rich harvest." John 12:24 AMP

THREE ESSENTIALS

Loved and known
A necessity
And belonging
A needful part of the three
Not just head knowledge
But received in the heart
Amazingly sets us free.

Vigorous and vital
A life-giving necessity
God's love the essential oil
Healing streams of love absorbed
Soothing all dis~eases
Applied often..... day or night
Eases all the issues of life
Binding up and healing..... as needed.

Nourished with love
Skillfully applied
Comfort..... not from a bottle
But God Himself, the Supplier and Source
An effervescent fountain
Never running dry
Making sure you have a good supply
Always available
He will abundantly fill the order.
Apply generously.
A guaranteed revival.

ODE TO TIME

Time is ticking by . . . . . oh so quickly
With not a minute to spare
Now it is here
Now it is gone
Never to reappear.

So . . . . . where does time go?
It doesn't have two feet to run
We can't see wings
But time does fly away
Where?

I look up to the sky
Time didn't take time to say goodbye
I heard no sound
Just . . . . . gone.

MY DOLL

I found a picture of a doll one day
Just like mine from years ago
A doll..... O so loved and precious
One that had really mattered
Quickly I knew what I had to do
A rescue..... was in order.

Rushing to the give-away box in my daughter's garage
I picked her up, holding her ever so close
So old, so worn, so cracked and broken
I knew I could not, would not let her go.

Memories of my little girl heart
Who sought to care, to give, to love, be loved
To belong and matter
Now found herself like her doll..... old and tattered.

If one feels broken, lost, cast off and rejected
A body wasted just like my old doll
Do not succumb to dreams broken
As though this is all there is to life in the here and now.

There is One Who knows us and loves us
Will rescue, reclaim, restore us from the box we are in
To pick us up with great joy and delight
Whatever condition we are in.

Just as I found..... and my doll found
Good News for you too!
For this..... Jesus came
To love and take care of you.

A DAY TO REJOICE

A unique design
Just one of a kind
That's YOU.

The day of your birth
Caused rejoicing on earth
The angels in heaven sang praise too
You caused such joy . . . . . and it still goes on
Making God's plan . . . . . a day to rejoice all life through.

May the blessings of God
Abundant each day
Cause your face to shine like the sun
He has kept you sound all these many years
Grace, love, mercy and peace . . . . . overwhelmingly yours
You have won.

Thank you Heavenly Father for your good idea
Lending us Your special gift from above
Heaven's delight became our sight
Happy day of this birth
Indeed . . . . . we celebrate . . . . . YOU!

"Before I formed you in the womb I knew you, before you were born I set you apart." Jeremiah 1:5

"Your eyes saw my unformed body. All the days ordained for me were written in your book before one of them came to be. How precious to me are your thoughts O God." Psalm 139:16,17 NIV

BIRTHDAYS

Where have all the years flown to
How can we be . . . . . "this old"
Father time has sounded the trumpet
Ready or not . . . . . another year did unfold.

When young . . . . . this was with eager anticipation
But now . . . . . we say stop the clock, put time on hold
So savor the moment with appreciation
Live life in the now . . . . . a moment at a time we are told.
One breath at a time is all we have
So enjoy each fleeting exposure
Aware of Love's intimate enclosure
Each moment, each encounter . . . . is of the Divine.

From the first breath as a new born baby
To the last breath however long the time
May we be aware of the love of our Savior
Seeking us . . . . . keeping us . . . . . being with us
All life long . . . . . all life through.

We are God's idea
He has offered us eternal life it is true
Complete in Him . . . . . the mission
Knowing Him is what He wants for me and you.

Happy day of your birth forever
Now that is a long, long time
Planned for in God's mind . . . . called and chosen
Before the heaven and earth was formed
Why then . . . . . that makes us older than dirt
An amazing thought to ponder at this time.

So . . . . . celebrating you
HAPPY BIRTHDAY since the beginning of time!

"Before I formed you in the womb I knew you, before you were born I set
you apart." Jeremiah 1:5

"Your eyes saw my unformed body. All the days ordained for me were
written in your book before one of them came to be. How precious to me
are your thoughts O God." Psalm 139: 16,17 NIV

THE UMBRELLA

Into each life. . . . . rain does fall
An umbrella, a useful cover
Will I use a black one
Or one with a multitude of bright color?

The rain. . . . .
Do I have hope and a joyful acceptance
Or despair, black all around I see
The choice of color for my umbrella
Could say a lot about me.

Depending upon how one looks at the rain or storms in life
And Who or what is my covering
The rain. . . . .
A replenishment. . . . . bringing new life
Or discouragement . . . . bleak, black, no hope,
ugliness in sight.

Is God my covering . . . . . invited into my rain
Or am I trying to go it alone
Like the umbrella. . . . . a choice I must make
As I walk through this life's storm.

MY BIRTHDAY FLOWERS

Oh,..... the beauty of my flowers
Such a gorgeous display
Magnificent roses stately stand
Three yellow tulips too
Purple stock with a fragrant smile
Orange day lilies opening new each day
A vibrant hot pink gerber daisy
Tucked inside too
And amidst all the beauty
God's love shines through.

Dear Tim and Jolie
Thank you for my flowers
Sent to bring me birthday joy
They have achieved your goal
I just wanted to say thank you
And tell you so.

EMILY GRACE

In the twenty years since God gave you breath
We have seen a life of grace unfolding
A main event..... your baptism stated
You gave your heart to God..... nothing withholding.

A merry heart..... good medicine it is true
Has generously blessed and ruled God's call on you
Giving of yourself and your substance
A heart of love and kindness
Abundantly poured out to all through you.

Running the race that was set before you
Taking strong hold of opportunity as it came along
Your character being formed in the midst of your choices
Proclaimed God's glory..... with thanksgiving..... and song.

Emily, you found great joy in stitching
Sewing machine going full speed ahead
Items of love joyfully made
Then generously given away as you felt led
Whether cleaning up the office or delighting in child care
Or serving Fruitive with amazing organizational flair
Emily, you gave a part of your heart for all the world to share.

A world traveler..... with wings on your feet
Alone..... and off to China at seventeen
Two trips to Uganda serving the Lord
A fun trip to Hawaii..... Alaska, too
Most amazing..... all that you do!

Learning obedience and trust through the things you
have suffered
Rooting and grounding your life to answer God's call
God entrusting you to follow in faith believing
Encouraging your heart in the midst of it all.

Given strength in exchange for weakness

Hope and comfort to walk and not fall
Grace to continue, humility, and courage made real
God's loving care for you in these short twenty years
And now for many more.

So privileged to share my heart with you dear granddaughter
And amazing to me the same birthdate, too
Surely goodness and mercy have followed us
And eternity is planned for us too.

So dear Emily~~~God will continue to bless and keep you
Showing you His will and His way
Holding you ever close to hear His heart
Always loving you..... never leaving you
Being with you
Day after day.

Happy day of your birth..... forever!
Great joy and love to fill and overflow your heart
Fulfilling God's great pleasure
You, Emily Grace are a special treasure.
Loved..... always

AT PEACE ON THE EASTERN SHORE

Sitting by the sea shore
Watching the waves roll in
Seagulls soaring and circling
Scouting for a morsel
Then touching down on the sand
Finding what had fallen
From an unknown generous hand.

They do not fret or worry
Concerned about their food supply
But do often fuss and chatter
When another bird with something in his mouth flies by.

The wind is causing whitecaps
A soothing roar to my ears
Thankful that I can watch at a distance
Just sitting, enjoying a peace within.

So far and no further
The line for the water has been set
Safe behind the sea wall
I know I won't get wet.

But should the winds get stronger
Causing a mist to spray
I will still stay longer
Enjoying the sun-filled day.

Come and join me sitting
We need not speak above the roar
Just enjoy the time together
Quietly observing and rocking
Letting our imaginations soar
At peace . . . . . on the Eastern Shore.

SEED

When the raindrops fall
And water the earth
Seeds smile below the surface
Ready to sprout
When the sun comes out
Waiting to break through the surface.

Seeds planted too
In our garden called life
Bear fruit..... or is a weed to be plucked out
A choice to be made
What to do when it grows
Will it stay
Must it go
For surely the decision will show.

"Happy and fortunate are you who cast your seed upon all waters when
the rivers overflows its banks; for the seed will sink into the mud and
when the waters subside, the plant will spring up; you will find it after
many days and reap and abundant harvest), you who safely send forth
the ox and the donkey (to range freely)." Isaiah 32:20 AMP

A LEAF

A leaf drifts slowly to the ground
Disconnected from its source of life.
What will happen now?

Nothing needs be lost in life it's true
Just looking for a new reason or season
Another point of view.

Children jumping in the many leaves that were gathered
Laughing with shouts of glee.
Small animals find a garment of protection
Hiding deep inside the pile so high.
Another purpose and reason for being
Even though disconnected from the tree.

Each season of life brings challenge
From glorious beauty . . . . . to faded hue
From new life . . . . . great hope and expectation
To the last call that comes . . . . . all through.

So live life now to the fullest
Not in regret of the past
Each day is a gift before us
Unique . . . . . with potential to grasp.

Don't miss a single moment
Behind every cloud shines the sun
Thankfulness turns the tide of depression
And sends it back to hell on the run.

Believing in God's great goodness
Seeking Him for favor divine
As we age, He never leaves us
His hand I know . . . . . always connected to mine.
Not exclusive
He wants to be connected to you too.

HUMOR

Life..... a series of experiences
Shaping our character as it goes along
How will we handle its pitfalls
Holes so deep it is hard to go on.

Humor..... a comic divergence
Helping to soften the blows of life
A way of dealing with truth even of a hurtful nature
Making a way to accept..... not excuse
Or get discouraged with life's plight.

Just as a soft word turns away anger and wrath
As a spoonful of sugar helping bitter medicine go down
Humor is a welcome ally
Taking off sharp edges
Instead of a sigh, a moan or a groan.

A merry heart makes good medicine
The sun in a life experiencing great rain
God giving freedom to see another point of view
Not a yoke of despair or gloom..... but for our gain.

"Come to Me and I will give you rest" Jesus says
"Take My yoke upon you
Learn from me"
Remember I AM is with you
The source of joy
A song in the night.

AN OPPORTUNITY

A gift of affirmation
Lifts the spirit
Hugs the heart
Encouragement
Given straight from the Father's heart.

When we receive comfort this day
Now we can share it with others
Someone needs to hear kind words
To help them along their way.

A smile, a hello, looking another in the eye
Says I see you ..... you matter
Wishing you well this day
People hunger for a touch such as this
Feeling they belong
We have the privilege of having a part in giving them this.

All comfort and encouragement originates from God you see
Meant to be a building block
Between God and you and me.
All gifts received and are shared
Multiplies the joy
Give out and you will receive more
Bringing comfort and hope and joy to the soul being restored.

"Blessed be the God and Father of our Lord Jesus Christ, the Father of mercies and God of all comfort, who comforts us in all our affliction, so that we may be able to comfort those who are in any affliction with which we ourselves are comforted by God." 2 Corinthians 1:3,4 ESV

A LIGHT

The battle of the ages
The kingdom of darkness versus Light
Is going on all around us
Do we "see" the fight for life?

How dark can be that darkness
Even with eyes seemingly open wide
Except the Light Of The World
Comes and opens up spiritual eyes.

We don't know what we don't know
Nor see what we can't see
But if the Gospel be hidden
The blinding comes from Satan with glee.

Many, caught in his clutches
Believing the father of lies
Needing release from condemnation
And the bondage of sin from within.

The battle is upon us
Use weapons that can be brought to the fore
Call on the mighty name of Jesus
And the enemy you see . . . . . must flee . . . . . out the door.

Jesus used the Word of God
Defeating the enemy of the Light
So hide The Word in your heart
Speak it also
And the enemy must take flight.

Are you filled with Light from the Savior
Are you a luminary being used in the Master's plan
To dispel darkness and impending disaster
Reflecting His light of life and love wherever you can?
Are you?

STOP

I feel a tenseness in my body, Lord
I did not realize it was there
Not until I became quiet before you
And released it to your care
Did I find rest and peace inside
Once again, the fruit of being in Your Presence
You, Lord . . . . . making me aware.

There is something about stopping
If only acknowledging a need for a deep breath
Taking time to pause and reflect
Quietly apprehending what could be called . . . . .
Neglect.

Caught up in every day hurry
Not feeling or being aware of my lack and need
In loving kindness and Your mercy
You faithfully allured me back
So I would stop, indeed!

There is a time to press forward
Also a time to stop . . . . . take stock
Weak and heavy laden
You cannot stay on top.

Roll your cares on Him
He bids us to come and find
Rest in our labors
With His love and peace in mind.

AT ONE TIME

My soul..... detached from its moorings
Unsettled, disquieted
Not sensing I was fearful
Just..... alone.

Sitting on my couch feeling helpless
All I could say was "God help me"
Along with a cry, a sigh and a groan.

Now I did not know this was possible
That God was available and would help
But He set wheels in motion
And then . . . . I understood.

I have spent over half a century now
A recipient of His love, grace and understanding
Guiding me and teaching me
His hand in mine I know
Never leaving me ever
Until to heaven I go
With Him..... forever.
His!

ALONE

I do understand your loneliness
I've been there, too, before
Wanting to share myself with someone
Nobody there at the door.

Silently the room is speaking
A voice is needed within
It shouts so loud without a voice
Quietness fills the din.

Vain imagination
Does not fill the void
I must seek new friendship
And allow people back inside.

Giving out what you need for yourself
Is like the two loaves and fishes that multiplied
Enough to go around
Twelve baskets left over besides.

So, do not turn inward
Stretch forth your hand to be healed
The Master goes before us
His love for us is sealed.

Looking upward..... and onward
Listen for His call
Called to know and love Him
That is the best of all.

P. S. Do not submit to resigned sorrow.

POETRY

Poetry in the heart
Needing expression
Alive
Compelling
Vibrant
Lyrical
Reflecting
Soothing
Haunting
The soul ready to spill over
Cascading thoughts as rushing water over the dam
So powerful..... uncontainable
Ready to burst the dam
Billowing waves raging against the shore
An effervescing fountain of water
A meandering stream
Bubbling and babbling water singing over smooth stones
A river of life
Healing waters
Quieting visitations
Reflections like on still water.

WHAT DO I DO?

Friend, are you hurting?
Are you searching in the dark?
Are you at a crossroad in life
Wondering . . . . .wandering
Looking for light . . . . . and for sight?
Is your heart crying out
Longing for someone to care?

Have your self-effort resources given out
Not in good shape . . . . . bottomed out
And that to you has been made clear?
Are you feeling like a rubber band
Stretched . . . . . feel your breaking point is near?

Having been there, this is what I found.
As I called out to God, He reached down to me
Help . . . . . just a prayer away
I listened carefully and heard God say:
"I AM WITH YOU ALWAYS . . . . . DON'T DESPAIR
CALL ON ME . . . . . I WILL MAKE A WAY."

Isn't that good news when pressed to the max
An invitation to come . . . . . seek . . . . . and to find
Comfort, encouragement and all that we need
Our source . . . . . He will open the way.

WALKING

Walking through the valley of the shadow of death
Physically, emotionally and/or spiritually
You are with me.

Oh God, Your rod and staff they comfort me
Always desiring to lead and direct me
To Yourself.

Thank You.

YES, LORD

Lord Jesus, take my hand
Walk me through this weary land
I am parched and I am worn
And my heart is really torn
Help me up that I may stand . . . . . before You.

As You reach out to me
Saying, Come, come home to Me
"Nothing in my hand I bring
Simply to Your cross I cling"
Is the fact my heart declares . . . . . I need You!

I come, Lord Jesus. Yes, I come
Your sacrifice has set me free
Having purchased my life at Calvary
Forever and ever to be with Thee
Thank you.

Then all those in heaven and on earth rejoiced
Life with Jesus was the choice
Grace abounded . . . . . and joy resounded
Praising God for your life . . . . . now and eternally.

Written for Dee and Alden Avery . . . . and all those nearing home.

YOU, GOD, SEE ME

LORD
I don't understand
Why all of a sudden..... from out of the blue
My heart felt broken into pieces
Terribly sad and feeling great loss.

I have been alone so long
With no one to share deep inner thoughts with
You are the only One to whom I can go
So here I am before you.

Then it happened.....

Uninvited
Unexpected
Hiding beneath the surface
Submerged and covered over
With no planning, no forethought
Suddenly.....
Tears streamed down my cheeks
Like a raging river overflowing its banks.

Made aware of deep feelings
Precious hopes and seeds of great promise
That never seemed to bring fruit
Had long given way to despair
Holding me captive, a prisoner indeed
Shackled, suppressed, bound tight in my chest
Long clothed in silence
Now..... needing to be expressed

A release of emotions had just taken place
A gift unexpected. it's true.
God freed me from grief long carried
So my life could rebound, by turning it around
Using a gift of tears.

Once again . . . . .
Thank you, Lord, for meeting me
Seeing and knowing my greatest need at the moment
Union and communion with you, my God
Made possible through the Atonement.

Come fill my heart with Your perfect love
Great Lover of my soul
I come to You . . . . . I run to You
For healing and release to my soul.

Thank you for your gift of tears
Bringing freedom from pent-up emotions
In the desert of my life when I thought I was alone
Once again . . . . . I am in awe knowing
You, God, see me.

"For I satisfy the weary ones, and refresh every one who languishes." Jeremiah 31:25 NASB

But in all these things we overwhelmingly conquer through Him Who loved us. For I am convinced that neither death, nor life, nor angels, nor principalities, nor things present nor things to come, nor powers, nor height nor any other created being will be able to separate us from the love of God, which is in Christ Jesus our Lord." Romans 8:37-39 NASB

WANDERING

A wandering soul, feeling alone
Zig zagging through the wilderness of life
With eyes blinded by the evil one
Pride and arrogance becomes their guide.

Doing what is right in their own eyes
Self-effort and stubbornness their god
The error..... in walking this way
All end with the same plight
Dead men walking..... no spiritual life.

Separated from God, devoid of The Light
With no absolute truth to guide them
Human knowledge their sight
Putting up a good fight.....
To be right.

For those who have a form of godliness or religion
But deny the Power and the Source
Knowing facts but have no faith
Are spiritually dead....
Disconnected..... breathing, but no life.

To those in this condition
These statements may seem harsh
Intolerant..... dogmatic might be their cry.
You mean to say all will perish
Utter darkness to be their plight?
Yes, says the Word of God.

No matter how much we have prospered
Things ..... will never satisfy
Eventually all "stuff" will lead to despair
Wondering if there is more to life than this.

Be aware there is Someone Who does cares
And does not want to leave you there

Stricken . . . . . and all alone
On your own.
It is God . . . . .
Who knows you and loves you
His great desire is for you to know Him too.

Want to know God's plan and how much He loves you?

Contained in the Word, God's voice can be heard
The Bible, giving wisdom and instruction to guide
The Holy Spirit was sent to teach you
So God's word can fill your understanding with truth.

An invitation to you is extended
Offering abundant new life for you
Through Jesus Christ, the Son
Ask Him to show you
COME to Him . . . . . be born anew.

"Call unto Me and I will show you great and mighty things, fenced in and hidden, which you do not know.(. . . have not knowledge of and under-stand)." Jeremiah 33:3 AMP

WILL I?

Will I only give God my shattered hopes and wounds
of yesterday
Or will I also give Him the unknown of today
And tomorrow..... if it comes?
Will the Wonderful, Counselor, Mighty God, King of Kings
Be my reality this day?
Will I entrust it all to Him?
Will I?

Will I worship Him in sorrow
Or only in joy that He bestows?
Will I acknowledge His ownership
Submit and surrender myself to Him
Giving to Him all my hopes and cares and woes?
Will I?

Faith without seeing is the true bottom line
Will I believe in God's love for me
In spite of hard circumstances
Laying my self-life down and waiting before Him?
Knowing He did not/ will not depart from me
Will I?

Only in the throes of living life
Will I truly know what my answer will be
No pat answers or wishful thinking will suffice.
Faith untested is unreal
But when I cannot see a positive end, will I stretch
out my arms
And with all that is within me..... believe and seek Him?
Will I?

I must choose each day whom I will serve
A choice either making myself my god..... or Him
Brought to the endpoint that I am not in control
Once again, God..... I yield for You to make me whole.

Wholly yours..... nothing held back
Abiding in faith..... believing
Only you can fulfill my divine design
Once again.....
Yes,
I am willing.

YIELDED AND STILL

Lying on the operating room table
The Surgeon..... given permission and ready to explore
What was in that heart of mine
Plus reveal..... so much more.

Shock never crossed His face
But kindness and love filled His eyes
Knowing it was for my good
What needed to be excised.

Since out of the heart the mouth does speak
Expressing all the issues of life
Not only did I need a heart transplant
But a transformation of the mind.

His word..... like a bright laser beam
Cutting to the chase
Zeroes in with conviction..... and a cleansing stream
Needed by the whole human race.

Sometimes kicking, heels digging in
Not wanting to be confronted by my own way of sin
But when I stopped struggling..... started confessing
Yielded and still
His amazing love received
Then I could embrace more of Him
And be healed and transformed from within.

Over fifty years have gone by
This, being a life-long procedure
The Skillful Hand knowing just what is needed
Surgically astute..... always bringing me through
Generously giving me His loving-kindness, peace and joy
Enabling me to see and hear and become more like Him.

"The heart is deceitful above all things and beyond cure. Who can under-
stand it? I the Lord search the heart and examine the mind, to reward
a man according to his conduct, according to what his deeds deserve."
Jeremiah 17:9,10 NIV

73

"And I will give them one heart, and a new spirit I will put within them. I will remove the heart of stone from their flesh and give them a heart of flesh." Ezekiel 11:19 ESV

TOPSIDE ~ UNDERSIDE

Ever-rolling waves
Crashing on the shore
Caused by winds one cannot see
But results are seen in making white caps
Pushing on to shore.

Restless churning
Heard by the naked ear
Causing wonder in my mind
What is happening in the surface below
Why . . . . . it is non-existent fear
to the fish below.

Life is like that too
Sometimes rough the waves
The call to go deeper, deeper still
The Spirit leading and guiding us on
To a quiet peace in the deep
That God will lead us to.

"Trust in the Lord with all your heart, and do not lean on your own under-
standing. In all your ways acknowledge Him and He will make your paths
straight. Proverbs 3:5,6

WHAT LORD

LORD
What is my problem?
Why am I depressed?
I feel so tired
Should I go to bed and rest?
Or would that be just an escape
Of what is really bothering me
I am not sure I know
But definitely, ... I am feeling low.

Today is Veteran's Day
And 47 years ago
Gary's funeral on the 12th
To Arlington, a long line of cars would go.

His spirit went to be with you, Lord
His earth suit left behind
The smile that was upon his face
Said Your amazing love and peace he did find.

How I have longed for a father's arms
To be wrapped around my children
A gift of affirmation and love from Dad
Has not been their vision.

Feelings are neither right nor wrong
But . . . . . they just are
Longings looking to be fulfilled
No, they are not sin.

Feelings like these, come and go
Looks like I have given up on fulfillment here on earth
But knowing this is but an interlude . . . . . and just
being human
This, too, is a part of Your master plan.

Sometimes my heart does cry
Lord, O Lord..... take me with You to the sky
There is nothing on earth for me to hold onto
O God, my heart feels cold and my spirit..... dry?

O God, my King, revive my heart
Living water for my thirst
I yield myself to you once more
Knowing full well..... You will meet me again.

I have long asked that I may finish well
All you had planned for me
I know it is not for me to decide
The time my soul will flee.

Grace to stay
Grace to go
My times and life are in Your hand
Submitting all to You
I wait..... on You.

Thank You, Lord, for saving me
All those long years ago
I am thankful that You will speak to me
Your answer and Your call.

"Why are you in despair, Oh my soul? And why have you become disturbed within me? Hope in God, for I shall again praise Him for the help of His presence." Psalm 42:5 NASB

WEATHERING STORMS

The tide is in, the water dark
Waves..... huge..... white caps wildly rolling
Winds pushing them on
Set in motion..... ever coming.....non-stop
With anger they roar
Crashing against the shore.

Some storms of life are like that.

Remembering the Man in the boat one day
A fierce storm causing great fright
Jesus just spoke, "Peace be still."
The waves ceased, becoming meek as a lamb.

The power of God's Presence
His spoken word
Show even the winds must obey Him.

How thankful I am in my storms of life
I've invited that Man in my boat
Putting Him in charge, I now can sleep
Casting all my care upon Him.

Storms will come and storms will go
That..... I cannot control
But never alone..... and safe am I
A boundary set
So far..... and no further
Grateful, His child am I.

"And He awoke and rebuked the wind and said to the sea, 'Peace! Be still.' And the wind ceased, and there was a great calm." Mark 4:39 ESV

WHEN I AM OLD

When my legs and strength give out
And maybe I can no longer stand
Shackled, imprisoned, captive
Needing a Savior, eternal and near
To set things right and deliver from fear.

Stretched and pummeled though I may be
You, Jesus only, truly know me
Thank You, Lord, You will take me by the hand
Transport my mind to where skies are bluer still
Looking forward to the promised land . . . . . with You.
I will speak Your praise and honor the fact
You never deserted me and You always came through.

Help me, Lord
No whining
No "why me" victim spoken here
No "only in times past did I matter"
You have me now in the palm of Your hand
So help me, Lord, not to succumb to this kind of chatter.
Useless words . . . . indelibly etched
Will cut my soul in pieces.

How I treasured our intimate times together
When unable to do "it" whatever it was . . . . . myself
God made it known
Not just sometimes, but all of the time
He is my Strength, my Hope, my Healer and my Enabler.

Blessed are we who seek His face
Healing streams for the mind when needed
When seeing His child stuck in pain or loss
Wants His love to draw me close
To give me freedom in my soul
Joy to dance inside
Internal peace in my trial
Straight from God's heart to mine.

TIME OUT

Sitting on the garden bench
Entertaining clusters of thoughts
I spread my arms to gather them in
But alas, they are elusive and won't come in.

How can I quiet the momentum within
If the beauty of the garden isn't successful?
I find the busyness of my life
Has become a thief..... a robber..... a dis-stressor.

I see the butterfly fluttering about
Being strengthened by the flowers' sweet nectar
Sipping a little here, a little there
His thread-like feet gently landing.

I see the squirrel scurrying about
Planting nuts for a winter supply
What am I storing up?
My breath responds with a sigh.

The call of a cardinal
Flying from tree to tree
Is he speaking to his friend
Or trying to speak to me?

The beauty of the roses
Fragrant perfume filling the air
Exerting no effort, but...... just being there
Delighting the senses to those who are aware.

The bubbling of the fountain
Attracting birds and bees
Recipients of the water's refreshment
Inviting them..... come, drink from me.

They are all doing and going about
Living their life quite naturally.
Flaunting freedom in their ease and grace

Not needing to think, impress or comply
Just beautiful . . . . an example
Free to be.

Oh may the beauty of this garden
Invest itself in me
Quieting thoughts, beautiful thoughts
Becoming a part of me.

Something simple
Nothing grand
My life is called to be
Caught up in God's plan
Needing to allow His love to abundantly fill me.

No striving . . . . . just a gentle flow
His love . . . . . covering me like honey
Warm and close
With His hand in mine
Enjoying the peace and the beauty on display.

A special time out in God's garden
A resting place . . . . . a safe place
My thoughts now gathered
Peace will flow
My heart will know
My being . . . . . no longer scattered.

A MOMENTARY VIEW FROM A HEARSE

Awakened before 4:00 in the morning
And now it is 4:45
Is this the day that the music inside of me..... dies
Or is this just a season..... a part of life?

Feeling alone..... and Oh, so vulnerable inside
After a holiday high
Hearing and feeling the hurts of loved, wounded ones
crying out
Intense the feeling..... and pain
Like a sink hole of earth..... swallowing life.

The darkness of night has encompassed
Not able to see a light on the path
Seemingly nothing secure..... or long lasting
Hope..... out of sight..... taken flight.

The frailty of human nature
The sin that so readily besets
The agony of daily living at times
And so easy to get caught up in regret.

Except You breathe life into our bodies, O God
Restore the life in our frame
It is easy to believe the lie
I (and others) have lived this life..... in vain.

The frost on my heart
Is it frozen?
Unable to function
Its hope frozen too?
Hardly beating
Too much pain..... feeling broken in two.

Makes me question

Are you still sitting beside me?
With You..... is my life still in full view?

Or have you deserted me, Father
My life..... no longer with you?

Me..... sitting in the stillness
Breathing..... shallow and slow
Waiting..... watching..... life going by
Oh, the pain of this earth..... it is so.

Feelings..... neither right nor wrong
Can be unreliable, not always truth
But painful..... none the less
I see the tears, feel the hurts of others..... and my own
Heartache and strife that filled the night.

I cry out..... Oh God, help us to endure.
We are vulnerable..... a weak chosen vessel
Tempted by the devil
His mocking voice we hear
Undone..... often..... and without strength
Graceless.....hopeless..... helpless
Desperate..... empty..... restless
Without joy..... a terrible view.

Hope of all the ages
Come..... rekindle Your spark
How dark is this dark
Written on these pages

Help, God!

Emmanuel..... God with us
Provided when Glory came down
The angels declaring the message
Good will and peace
Love and encouragement, too
HE..... would fulfill.

Reminded of what He has told us
"For I know the plans I have for you
Not for evil, but for good

He is perfecting those things which concern us"
Giving us His point of view.

His ways are not our ways
His thoughts ..... higher than ours, too
He gives His Light in our night
His love to see us through.

We are called to stand with each other
Bonded by prayers out of faith
Reflectors of His love
Arms open wide ..... we give and take.

Really, ... there is no place to run
Or a need to hide
No hole so deep
His love does not find us
But ..... in HIM ..... we must abide.

Jesus bids us come
His yoke is easy, His burden is light
I know ..... He will carry our plight.
And walk us through our night.

Honestly, this was a view from the hearse in my life
Hauling my dead or dying thoughts around
But God's grace did not let me stay there
He gave another opportunity to die to self
To yield and see
Release ..... enabling me to go free
His grace I found.

Have you ever been there?
Are you there now?
Hope and help are available
Just a prayer away.

"Trust in the LORD with all you heart and do not lean on your own under-
standing. In *all* your ways submit to Him and *HE* will make your path
straight." Proverbs 3:5,6 NIV

SAIL ON!

The water is vast with turbulence
Far as the eye can see
Uncharted waters
Just my God and me.

He Who knows the beginning
And how the end will be
I will trust my Captain
As we sail across life's sea.

His strength exchanged for my weakness
His grace . . . . . sufficient for me
Difficulties You will remove when no longer needed
For my good . . . . . Your glory . . . . . and Your face to see.

Sail on! Sail on, O Captain
I will *learn* contentment with you at the helm
In weakness, distress and difficulties
That assail the whole human race.

Endured, persevered in all types of weather and trial
The Captain stays focused on His goal
Never asleep in my boat of life
Keeping me near . . . . . quieting my fear
Releasing me from being alarmed.

"I see the Lord is always before me. I will not be shaken for He is right
beside me. No wonder my heart is glad, And my tongue shouts His
praise! My body rests in hope." Acts 2: 25,26 NIV

ME

O my God and Heavenly Father
It is in **You** that I can trust
Please scoop me up and hold me
You know that I am but dust.

Most likely I was not wanted
Is what my heart does say
But that is not important
Because it is **You** Who made my way.

Your word has brought such an assurance
I am Your idea
Not of the will of man or the flesh
You planned for..... called and chose me
You have witnessed to my heart
I believe that is why I am alive this day.

You knitted me together..... in my mother's womb
Amazing truth so profound
This has indeed turned my life around
And I KNOW that I belong.

So thankful that I was not aborted
Without having a chance to live
So grateful for my children
You were so kind to me to give.

Called that I might know You
To bring Your heart great pleasure
Thank you, Lord, for saving me
A joy that is without measure.

All the circumstances of my life
Tailor made and properly fitting
To become a garment of praise
That I might rise up in thanksgiving.

Before I formed you in the womb I knew you, and before were born I con-
secrated you....." Jeremiah 1:5 RSV

IN LIGHT OF ETERNITY

When life is hard and painful
And questions fly like arrows through the air
When grief can seem unending
Questioning, "Why?" with many tears.

Lord Jesus, how You wept..... groaning in deep sorrow
Even knowing you would bring Lazarus back to life
Our human loss You felt..... identifying with our tears
When loved ones..... depart.

I have heard in acceptance lies peace
O God..... please help us do just that
Of anguish that goes deep
Sometimes..... seemingly with no relief.

Eternal life for us Your vision
When from the grave You arose
You were the Father's provision
Suffering and dying in our stead.

To those who have received You
Death overcome..... a victory..... forever true
No longer bound by earth's limitations
Unfettered..... set free..... all things become new.

For just a short time separation has come
But a glorious new day is in view
Endured..... persevered..... for the joy that is ours
Purchased by Jesus..... it is true!

The relationships we have
All..... bought with a price
A gift from God's hand to ours
Not ours alone..... all is on loan
Until just the right time..... You call us home.

So now a question that should be addressed
By each one this side of the grave

What would I give in exchange for my soul to have
Eternal life.....abundant life
Blessed by You and made whole?

Our sorrow..... not without purpose
Through tears of surrender I find
God is always there..... His heart of love to provide
Comfort..... and peace..... and strength to survive.

Constantly nourished by the living word each day
God's love letter to us..... showing us His way.
Do not let your heart be troubled
A choice..... that puts faith on display.

In a soon day, in a blink of the eye
Eternity will bid each of us..... come
But until then..... God, comfort us again, again and again
Your love and presence..... displayed.

LAZING AT THE BAY

The tide is out on Chesapeake Bay
Captured . . . . . a pool of warm water
Alluring me down to sit in a chair
And dangle my feet in the water.

A gentle breeze
Ripples on the pool
The sun . . . . . creating sparkling magic
To have missed all this, on a day such as this
Would have to be labeled . . . . . tragic.

So far and no further, a boundary was set
Waves lapping could not reach me.
A barrier between, a reminder comes through
A promise given by God, my Father.

So often in life, when storms rage strong
I remind myself of this promise
It is He Who sets limits, and is with me in it
I am safe . . . . . God, being fully in charge.

REMEMBERING MR. SNOWMAN

With a blank sheet of paper before me
Waiting to be filled
So says I, "Pen, where will we go today"?

Surveying the scene out the window
Memories flood toward me this day
Oh I know . . . . . West Virginia . . . . . and I am on my way.

Just beyond the horizon
Is a quiet place for me
I feel myself unwinding
As I drive to a place of rest.

Secure in a mountain hideaway
Far from hustle and bustle
I find time to breathe, time to reflect
Time to ease my cares from me.

Remembering the week of the snowfall
Sequestered by three feet of snow
The quiet, so deafening around me
How wonderful with no place to go.

The snow, glistening in the sunlight
So white . . . . . and so pure
Eventually said, "Come find me,
There is a snowman sleeping in here."

So out I went in the deep of the snow
Preparing a ball nice and round
I rolled it and rolled it and then found
Surprise, Mr. Snowman was found.

We both were so happy to find each other
A day of fun and glee
But then Mr. Sun came out to play
And dear Mr. Snowman had to flee.

He ran away while I wasn't looking
But I never will forget
The fun we had that crisp winter day
When all the earth was at rest
The joy that we found as we scurried around
And shared the beauty of the day.

A FEATHER

Feather in the wind
Flying high in the sky
Gracefully fluttering back to earth
Your flight..... drawing nigh.

But suddenly..... the breeze comes again
And lifting you high once more
You can dream you are an eagle's wing
As you soar....and soar....and soar.

Now as the breeze begins to wane
And you make your final descent
Wondering why you were at all
And what was my intent?

A little boy comes down the path
As happy as can be
For he sees you within his view
And knows you will be his treasure indeed!

You barely had time to land
And the little boy had you in his hand
Smiling in pleasure, captivated for sure
His imagination now active and running.

Sometimes an Indian
Sometimes a bird on the wing
Once a tickler running up and down his arm
But always so careful, not to cause you any harm.

You thought you were useless
But you arrived in the right hand
A reclaimed purpose spoken loud and clear
The boy exclaimed, "Dear feather,
I'm so glad that you are here!"

You thought your life had ended
But with a dreamer you see
Little feather, your life was revived
And you were gleefully..... set free

FOREVER

Forever..... a long, long, long time
Far beyond the journey of one's imagination
Or what we can see
God in His loving kindness
Planned eternity for you and me.

Needing no consultation
God spoke..... and it was done
The earth and planets set in proper rotation
Life had now begun.

Eternity..... placed in the heart of God's creation
Fashioned by His loving hand
Giving our restless heart a longing
For yet another land.

Knowing full well our frailty
A desire to run life our own way
With pitfalls of sin and temptation
Separating us from Him day after day.

God provided a way of forgiveness
To bring us back to Himself
The heart and love of our Father made flesh
Jesus...... .Dying in our stead.

And to all who would repent
Believe..... taking God at His Word
Receive His profound gift
Eternal life was found.
And now..... heaven-bound!

No more tears or groaning there
Not weighed down by the consequences of sin
But a peace and joy in His presence
Pleasures *FOREVER*..... being with Him.

".... He has also set eternity in their heart." Ecclesiastes 3:11(b) NASB

A GATEWAY

Sometimes our moments of greatest need
Are gateways to bring God close
When cries of "help" go out
"God, please rescue me."

God in His mercy
Protection and provision
I, in my need
Casting all my care on Him.

God in His loving kindness
Asking Him to bring it to bear on me
Not to negotiate or try to manipulate God
I must leave the method to Him.

His ways are not my ways
His plans for me..... always the best
A great exchange takes place
Then my soul will be at rest.

"For I know the plans I have for you, says the Lord.
Plans to prosper and not to harm you, plans
to give you a hope and a future."
Jeremiah 29:11 NIV

SPRING

Oh . . . . . a sweet bouquet of daffodils
Fragrant, majestic, bright yellow
Heralding the arrival of spring
Warm earth . . . . . new life
A breath-taking scene.

Birds returning to build their nests
Singing songs with great joy
Soon little peeps will fill the air
"Come quickly!
Time to eat . . . . . again".

Puddles of water
From rain replenishing the earth
Find children expressing their glee
Jumping up and down
Splashing in the muddy puddles joyfully.

New life . . . . . knows no bounds
Everything on earth is touched
Hope and beauty spring up with great declaration
That time when what is hidden will be set free
God's jubilee for you and me!
Welcome Spring!

HELP!

God, please help me
Stunned, I feel as though I am losing my way
Going through the motions
Seeing life with a lot of decay.

Lives once stable
Now shaken to the core
Darkness having pitched a tent
Sight..... now disabled.

A decision hastily made
Causing a major stumble
Lives forever changed
Cannot hide under a table.

Tossed and torn..... what to do?
Life's quick sand..... engulfing
Fright brought to light
Paralyzing gloom.

Oh my God, I am so helpless
My friend hurting so today
I know I cannot change the outcome
Please show her (and them) the way.

Blinded..... caught up in sin's allurement
Causes so much hurt and harm
Raging storms, swamped sinking boats
Jesus, you alone can save and guide us
Hear our alarm.

Certainly the answer to all this trial
Is not within ourselves
We must seek from You the answer
Trust and faith in You, God
There is no one or anything else.

Help!

"The eternal God is your dwelling place and underneath are the ever-lasting arms." Deuteronomy 33:27 ESV

MY EYE

I was looking at the speck
in my brother's eye
And found I had a beam in my own
Criticize and judge him.....
I better not
I must first extract the log from my own.

Then..... *maybe, just maybe* I can see
To help him out
But now with an eye
Humbled..... and with much-needed compassion.

Gently..... must need be
So we both can see
Truth or correction..... in a loving fashion.

MY PSALM

For His steadfast love and mercy endures forever!

An invitation to weary and heavy laden travelers
Pressed down by the trials of life
No fear in the midst of God's presence
But peace, a quiet retreat..... to commune.

You are forever to me a refuge
A high tower to Whom I may run
A safe place..... a resting place
To regroup..... and be met by The Son.

For His steadfast love and mercy endures forever!

Fifty years of traveling this highway
When the Savior became mine all those years long ago
We have tramped and trudged through the trenches
I thank You, God..... not alone.
There is no other reason for my being alive
Without Him, I do not believe I would have survived.

Numerically, over three quarters of a century might seem like
a very long time
But no need to count the years gone by
We were planned for, called out, conceived in His mind's eye
Before He made the heavens and the earth.
Making us all then..... older than dirt.

His steadfast love and mercy endures forever!

So if by design I hang around a little longer
New lessons He has for me I know
Not one minute too soon or much later
But submitting my life at His feet
I rest my case before Him
I will not see defeat.

The steadfast love of the Lord never changes

His mercies . . . . . new every day
The Word of God never fails us
But endures, day after day after day.

So best we not be weary in well doing
But walk through life with a grateful heart
Knowing that the Lord rewards us
Bringing joy . . . . . His hope . . . . . and His heart.

So help me to finish strongly my God
Holy Spirit, fill my heart with new wine
As long as I can wiggle
I must stay hooked to The Vine.

Precious children the Son has brought to The Father
So that now we can become the children of God
And the Father has given the Son His bride
For all eternity . . . . . never to depart.

My bridal dress is ready to wear
The oil in my lamp . . . . . all full
My Bridegroom will come at just the right time
What a great celebration will be held . . . . . that is true!

Or, maybe we will be caught up and meet in the air
Saints in heaven rejoicing
As we all gather there.

Even so, come quickly Lord Jesus
All on earth, You hear their moan and groan
Waiting for that great reunion
When you bring us before Your throne.

His steadfast love and mercy endures forever.

READY?

As the ravages of age take over
Bodies in the state of decline
Do we know Jesus as our Lord and Savior
Who is able to call us at any time?

We never know when that time will come
Be we young or be we old
It is important to be ready
That's why this poem is told.

I have no fear of death with Jesus
He walks with me through the sands of time
Whether in pain..... or suddenly
When my last breath is taken away
I am comforted in my knowing
I am His and He is mine.

Now to be absent from my body
Is to be present with my Lord
In one of His many mansions
Prepared above for His children with love.

Joy unspeakable is my transit
Praise the Lord, I am ready to go now..... or stay
Never did He ever leave me
And I now come to say
You, too, can receive Jesus as your Savior
Repent, yield your life to Him
And know with full assurance of faith
That you belong to Him.

His arms wide open to receive us
Glory fills our soul
At just the right time God will make us
Joyously well..... and whole.

Are you ready?

A LONGING

There is a deep, deep longing
Looking to be satisfied
My arms reach out to you, O God
To draw me to Your side.

To hold me, enfold me
To let me rest my head on You
There is no place else to go, dear Lord
Your love I need it is true.

I've never walked this road before
I cannot see the end
All I know is, I need You Lord
My Lover and Best Friend.

There is a quietness in this longing, Lord
Not frantic, or anxious . . . . . just is
A steady pull upon my heart
A longing . . . . . to be all His.

My life, a boat upon the sea of life
Sometimes storms blowing beyond measure
But always You, The Captain of my ship
To anchor me, with pleasure.

I am not left to drift along
Caught by a current with no direction
But manned by the mighty hand of God
His port of call for me . . . . . protection.

O longing, deep longing
Deep calling unto deep
My Captain, dear Captain
Safe in Your arms I will sleep.

Hitherto I lift my Ebenezer
Knowing well to whom I run
He will help me
It's His nature
When to Him I call and come.

Psalm 42 visitation

101

ONE FALL EVENING

Sitting on the porch rocker
Listening to the cricket chorus singing away
Rain once more gently falling
Musically pattering on the tin roof.

Leaves all wet and shiny
On the trees, the shrubs and flowers
I see the last rose of summer
Fall has already arrived with honors.

Remembering times like this from home long ago
Nostalgia sweeping through my thoughts
What would complete the picture?
Hearing the train
The haunting sound of the horn in the distance
Woefully declaring "caution. I'm about to cross the road".

It is good to take time to stop and listen
Enjoying the chorus, the remembrance and the view
Rocking through this fall evening
How I wish you were here too.

Nostalgia at Tim and Jolie's.

A VIEW

Looking out of the window
What do I see
Mountains..... partially covered with snow.

The sun is just rising
A big ball of red
There is frost on the roof and the trees.

I scan the horizon
Now what do I see
A hot air balloon..... and it is 28 degrees!

Who would be out
On a brisk morn like this
Must be an adventurer bundled up
Hoping not to freeze.

On further inspection
An amazing detection
A huge distant satellite dish had played a trick on me.

What a good way to start the day
A good laugh, a merry heart making good medicine
And a reminder that what we "see"
Is not always what it is
So a need to be open..... looking carefully
And maybe looking once again.

But wait..... I do take another look
After an hour has gone by
This time..... It is real
A hot air balloon really is flying in the sky.

So..... *keep* looking up
You might find an unexpected treasure
To give a lift like I found
An almost missed..... pleasure.

Park City, Utah

HORSESHOE CRABS

Dear Jonathan.....
The horseshoe crab
That brought you such joy
And caused a great stir in your spirit
Brought a smile to my face
As you scurried place to place
Bringing back three more
Now was that the limit?

Lying dormant on the beach
For such a time as this
Waiting for you as its destination.
With your creative juices flowing
Makes me wonder..... just how will you use them.
But there is no doubt in my mind
With your creative design
It will be amazing.

You let me inside
The spot in your heart
Where horseshoe crabs brought you such pleasure.
The excitement you found
Caused my heart to abound
The joy shown on your face..... my gift.

Simple pleasures shared
Joy with great abandon
Enabled me to share in their greatness too.

Thank you, dear Jonathan
For being so free
With a gift so rare
It allowed me to see..... and share.

A MINUTE'S RETREAT

In the hustle and bustle of a busy life
Stop . . . . . take time to breathe
Allow this quietness to gather your thoughts
To release the pressure within.

God is with you . . . . . listen . . . . . hear His voice
He will lead you to make the right choice
To all who come, He says enter in
Receive my peace and rest . . . . . within.

"It is I", says God, "who will put a smile on your face
Making your heart feel glad
As you reflect on the promises in my great Book
I have given you to have".

A minute's retreat will soothe your soul
Great comfort have they who do it
In His presence is fullness of joy
Be blessed . . . . . enter in . . . . . focus on Him
Be encouraged . . . . .
Do it.

"Be still and know that I am God." Psalm 46:10 ESV

AMAZING NIGHT

Love came down from heaven
Glory filled the earth
The long awaited Promised One, God's own Son
Jesus Christ our Savior
Became sight that amazing night.

Jesus showed us the Father's love
Abundant and never ending
Emmanuel, God with us
His love to us descending.

Jesus brought us such good news
Forgiveness and eternal life . . . . . His offer
Through His life and death and resurrection power
To be made one with Him . . . . . and the Father.

To all who receive this Gift
Love, joy, and peace
Grace and mercy is ours too
Heavens gates He did open wide
Have you received His loving invitation to you?

Time is of the essence now
Each day . . . . . quickly fleeting
Draw nigh to Him
Give Him your heart
Know He will draw near to you
His promised Holy Spirit will always be with you
Never alone.

RECLAIMED

My hands outstretched like a cup
Eyes closed
Quiet
Expectant
Having asked
Waiting on God to fill up my cup.

Dreams that had evaporated
Without saying goodbye
An invitation extended . . . . . come again
I would gather you in.

Joy exclusively mine
Enjoying the possibility
Whimsically
Not to be totally defined
Hope unearthed
New life and dreams mine
Once again . . . . .
Reclaimed.

Faith abiding
Restoration on the way.

THE HOPE OF SPRINGTIME

When the quiet comes
Stilling my soul
When Peace like a river
comes to make me whole
The Hope of springtime
captures my sight
To bring into focus
that which is right.

Old things have passed away
Released . . . . . yes, it is true
Enabling me to experience
another point of view
To celebrate life
Refreshed . . . . . born anew
With Hope in my heart
to enable me to go through.

Seasons of life
They have come . . . . . They have gone
Enable me, my God,
To finish strong.
Eternity has been written
into the heart of man
You have a loving . . . . . amazing plan.

The beauty of springtime
A harbinger of heaven
A foretaste of beauty
Inviting us
Come, ... enter in.

DUPED!

A trademark maneuver of Satan
A pleasure..... looking and feeling O so good!
Temptation making such an appealing offering
A high like we've never been on
Only to find it delivers something completely different
Dismayed
Our feet in a web..... caught
Becoming a prisoner in it.

Be on guard!

DEFEATED

Enemy of my soul
I am no longer in your control
Pressed down by your finger of darkness
That which had been hidden
Has been confessed to the Light
Now no longer a fight or a fright.

You are a lion with no teeth
Pitifully roaring at my feet
You have no right, no claim on me
The blood of Jesus says you must flee from me.

When I confess my sin and forgiveness takes place
There is nothing between God and me and the whole
human race
I have the freedom to breathe in peace
Pure freedom and delight
Jesus having won the battle for me.

DESTINATION

From the womb
To the tomb
We are God's creation and idea.

Made in His image
Each..... a unique design
Made for His glory
Each breath..... a gift just in time.

A desire for eternity
Built within each soul
The whole earth groaning and restless
Awaiting redemption of our soul.

RESPONSES

When you have been wounded
Do you want to hurt back?
Or does your response take a different direction instead?
Is it internalized with "what did I do?"
Placing the blame on you?

We all do something
Dealing with life's hurts
Strike out..... Shut down
Blame me..... Or blame you.
Stewing and stirring with a lot of self-talk
Hot tears, coldness and other emotions, too.

These choices are not the answer
Resolution and healing will not come
Hiding, imbibing, medicating of one sort or another
Ends up in wounding, too.

So..... What to do?
Pain seeks to have a voice, too.

Faced with choices..... not easy to make
Involves the will..... not easy to break
Will wants to be in charge..... no matter what
Haughty and proud, standing its ground.

The answer could come quickly
But with me..... most likely not
Nursing the festering wound
Churns the stomach into a knot.

Oh God, I am sorry
I know how important it is to keep short accounts.
Confront the issue
Get it straightened out.

The power of forgiveness
As Jesus has given is ours for today
Reconciliation might come
If we choose His way.

OUR TIMES

Brought to our wit's end
Needing God's affirming point of view
How life-giving the word of God
Enabling us to walk through.

Holy Spirit, make real the word
Overwhelm us with the truth
To endure, persevere, find rest in the midst
Till we can see..... not run
We come to You.

No, we can't pull ourselves up and out of this on our own
Pain..... so very real
Afflicted, perplexed, struck down
But not crushed, not in despair, not destroyed
No matter how it may feel

Fixing our eyes upon Jesus
The Author and Finisher of our faith
Strengthen our feeble knees
As we storm heaven's gate.

Underneath all the circumstances
God's almighty arms and power
Holding, keeping, loving, safe, always with us
Promises He will not fail to keep
Surrounded by so great a cloud of witnesses
Cheering us on
We lay it all..... at His feet.

"We are afflicted in every way, but not crushed; perplexed, but not driven
to despair; persecuted, but not forsaken; struck down, but not destroyed;
always carrying in the body the death of Jesus, so that the life of Jesus
may also be manifested in our bodies." 2 Corinthians 4:8-10 ESV

A BATTLE

A battle with depression
Makes a body feel old
The light of the eyes, the window of the soul
Grow dim.

Most times depression arrives
Uninvited and unannounced for sure
Caught..... unaware
Like a fly in a spider web.

I cry out.....
"Why are you cast down, O my soul?
Does anyone know.... or care?
And how did I get there"?

Now a seed had been planted
In the soil of my soul
Waiting for just the right time to grow
When tired, hungry, weak and alone
The conditions, just right
Self-pity wants to make a home.

Feeling overcome..... undone
Slammed with great sorrow
Anxious, without hope..... despair
Oh friend,..... have you ever been there?

A battle is raging
Waged by the enemy of our soul
His plan..... to dethrone God in our heart
To question, to doubt, to steal, to kill, to cause pain his goal.

Found in that condition, a trumpet sound of hope
Came through loud and clear to my heart.
Help from a Psalmist who had gone long before
Expressing,"Why must I go about mourning
Oppressed by the enemy of my soul?"

Desperate and brought low
A request went out from his mouth
Asking God to send light and truth to lead and guide him
To where God dwells.

Thirsting for God . . . . . needing His hope
Brought a new focus into view
Whom have I in heaven but You
And earth has nothing that I desire besides You.

It wasn't instant . . . . . the answer
But the clarion call and answer from God did come
Remember . . . . . and return to ME.
Come.

Revealing his heart by admission
Choosing this position, the Psalmist declared,
"I have made the Sovereign Lord my refuge, my hope."
How about me . . . . . and you . . . . . is that true?

The content and expression of his words
Now so different indeed!
So listen . . . . . Hear . . . . . See
How his life had turned around.

"Why my soul, are you downcast?
Why so disturbed in me?
Put your hope in God.
For I will yet praise Him,
My Savior and my God."
"I will tell of all your deeds".

So what does this say for me . . . . . and for you to do
If we find ourselves in this condition?
Remember . . . . . and return
Rehearse God's goodness
Give praise
And believing what God says,
The tide of depression is turned and defeated

The prisoner..... released from its hold and set free.

God inhabits the praise of His people.
So again..... and again..... and again when needed
Always turn to God and into His Word
His Spirit giving *us* sight
Leading and guiding
Through the utter darkness and into the Light
Bringing comfort and encouragement
Full of hope..... breathing into us..... new life.

Psalm 73:28 NIV; Psalm 42:11 NIV

CRUCIAL THE ANSWER

Life in the living
To what..... to Whom am I submitting?
A black hole
A hope so
A determined destination
Or to just being out of control?
Crucial the answer.

Intensity. Urgency.
Crisis. Laid back. Or nothing at all
Crucial the answer?

I found
The Love that knew me
Embraced and magnetically drew me
Stands . . . . knocking at the door of our heart.

Will I invite Him in
Wanting to be free from all sorts of sin
Bound to defeat me from within?
Crucial the answer.

I stand amazed
The love that God pours out
Day after day..... time after time
Onto a faithless, rebellious
"I want it my way"
Person.

Will I submit?
Will I answer,
"Come in" to The King of Love at the door?
Crucial the answer!

THOUGHTS

Our thoughts are not written with invisible ink
They become etched in the computer of our mind
Definite impressions become a part of the fabric of our life
Making us stable . . . . . or disabled
Broken . . . . . or whole.

So, take in truth
Reject lies whenever they are found
God's word is truth
Take it in . . . . . and abound.

God has told us who we are
And what His plan is for us
That we might know Him as He is
And belong to Him . . . . . forever.

Grace, mercy and peace have kissed our lips
When in love, Jesus becomes our Savior
His life, sacrificed for our sin
Enabling us to become one with Him and the Father.

Jesus is Lord of the living and the dead
Our opinions do not change fact
One day every knee will bow proclaiming this truth
To the glory of God, our Father.

THE VALLEY

When walking through the valley
The shadow of death lurking upon what I hold dear
What to do
How to see
Oh God, revive my soul, my plea.

Taking time to feel
Not repressing pain's claim
But facing it head on
Your peace again I claim.

Grace, mercy and peace
Having momentarily escaped
Draw me once again
I am humbled . . . . . on my face.

What one cannot fix
Or change the outcome of at all
Provides a platform for grace
Yes, on You, God . . . . . we must call.

Will I wait and trust in You
For strength and peace to come?
Past experiences have shown me
There is no other place to run.

Fill my cup with more of You, Lord
With love and understanding
I belong and yield myself up to you, Lord
Your invitation so commanding . . . . . Come.

You say, "Come and find ME
Adequate for your needs
Joy and peace residing
My love to set you free
I am with you always
To comfort and to guide

Never, ever to leave you
Available..... always by your side
Abide in ME"

Live..... encouraged.

CAPTURED

In that great chasm of aloneness
Just my Lord and me
He sees my inner depth, the unplowed ground
And what is needed for me to be
Fully enveloped in His plan
For what He wants to do in and through me.

As I ran in all directions
Hither and thither, to and fro
Just not knowing which way to go
His hand of love captured me.

Stopped by Love
So calming . . . . . and so assuring.
Succumbed by Love
So tender and endearing
Given life by Love . . . . .
I yielded.

Causing me to **hear** His voice
His first step in my knowing.
Enabling me to **receive** His love
His next step in His showing
Receiving His Spirit in all His fulness
Gifted me with potential
Granting me eyes to see . . . . . ears to hear
Love, joy and peace beyond belief to receive
So I could relinquish my life to Him
Be set apart for Him
Learn of Him . . . . . and
Know Him . . . . . Not just know *about* Him.

God spoke these words to my heart
and now I know . . . . .

All that you have is from My hand
See how lavishly I give

Good measure, shaken down and running over
So generously, hilariously you may live.

You are My good idea
I have tested you, it's true
To see what is in your heart
And with it all..... what you would do.

Questions..... questions..... questions
Heart issues come to the fore
Do you only trust Me because of what you see?
Or does your faith go down deeper to the very heart of Me?
Have you cultivated My word in your heart
Planted..... alive with good seed?

So says I as we walked down life's road
And I learned to know and trust Him more and more
"With Your hand on mine
Set the Plow point deep
Breaking up the stoney places in my heart
Unyielding..... stubborn..... no other way
Yes..... I want The Plow to have His way."

Breaking up the soil in my hardness of heart
Has caused me pain..... it is true.
But when given a vision, it is my decision
I want that Plow go through.

You Who see my inner depths,
Your plans for me are good
Planting seeds of righteousness
With a hearty harvest in view
That..... that is what I want You to do.

Planting good seed
I fertilize and water
The Word..... makes excellent rain.
I wait..... a good season
On God is the reason

He yields up good fruit in its time.

So..... instructions came
Occupy.
Be about My business until I return or call you home
Fear not to step out
Giving birth to what I have already done through My Son.

HERE AM I

No matter what I am doing
No matter what my age
Will I answer God's call on my life with a
"Here am I, Lord, send me"?

Whether it be across the sea
Or here at home to stay
My life is Yours O Lord
To use in any way.

Nothing in my hand to cling
All I have is Yours
Getting alone with you, my God
Speak to me within.

Seek, knock, find
I desire to know Your will
I wait on you to open the door
My life with You . . . . . praise God . . . . . forever more.

Knowledge only . . . . . pride puffs up
Can an idol be
Religion . . . . . a stumbling block
Union and communion with You
Needs to be what I seek for me.

Many years of "trying"
Thinking I could live life on my own
Provided many holes to fall in
Lessons learned and relearned
Now . . . . . humbled before Your throne.

So, yielded and still before you
My strength and confidence in You
To lead me and to guide me
Your word is always true.

My answer to God's call
Here am I
Send me!

IN THE FOG

It is a new day dawning
In spite of the mist and fog outside
By faith I know
For just a little while
The sun has gone away to hide

Hidden from my sight
Does not make it any less real
The sun is shining someplace
Above the fog . . . . . and it is real.

Times such as these remind me
How pleased and thankful I will be
When the sun once more comes back from hiding
And shines its light on me.

Just as Jesus said, "I must go away
But for just a little while
But someday I will return again"
On this fact I can believe . . . . . and smile.

Sometimes hidden
Sometimes perfectly seen
God has never left me
I am always on His radar screen.

Faith is tested when sight is not given
And like the fog that will soon pass away
In believing that His word is true
Not blind faith without reason
Our God of hope gives a vision
His heart speaking volumes to me and you.

HEALING DEEP WOUNDS

Brokenness, deep wounds occur in everyone's life
But putting bandaids on emotional or spiritual problems
Or ignoring them altogether
Will not send them away
Healing comes by dealing with the cause . . . . . God's way.

Sometimes the cause is a sin issue of one's own making
Or someone else has crossed a line
Sometimes damage occurs so early in life
Recall is difficult . . . . . or no awareness at all.
Deep level healing is needed here
Holy Spirit, I am calling on You to reveal what is needed
Spirit, body, mind, emotion and will.

Apply the resurrection power of Jesus to these
Touch the wound or memory with Your finger of love
For freedom, recovery and release.

Reveal negative attitudes
Give grace to forgive and to let go
Holding onto anger, hatred, bitterness, resentment,
Fear, shame, guilt, self-rejection, self-hatred, death wishes
And the list could go on and on
All affecting our relationship with God and others
A prison house all of its own
Festering, causing problems
Serious as the original wound.

Harbored attitudes such as these
Incite internal damage
Physically, mentally and spiritually
Extreme harm is done.

Negative attitudes toward ourself
In spite of the value God puts on us
A value we often know only in our heads
God wants in our hearts instead.

Lord Jesus, You called Your twelve disciples
Giving them power and authority to proclaim the
kingdom of God
Deliverance from demons
Heal diseases
So help is here, Holy Spirit teach us how.

Failure to see the extent God chose to limit Himself
By granting free will to all human beings
Satan, and the garbage that results from sin
Consequences of what people choose
Holding anger towards God
Because of the things one has suffered
Help is here . . . . . offer it all back to Him.

Satan plants and tells a lie
And if we keep rehearsing it
A habit is formed . . . . . difficult to break
Keeping negative attitudes and actions in place.

Choose life . . . . . choose against these strongly held lies
Jesus has shown the way to help
Give Him His rightful place
He will give amazing grace.

Being a partner with God
Opens the door to make all things work together for our good
But unless we call on Him
He does not push His way in.

Free will has been given to all.

God's will is always to save
But only to those who agree
He honors the choice of those who refuse His offer
How significant is our answer to Him.

Invited to choose this day whom you will serve
If God be God, serve Him
Anything less makes me my god
Another problem within.

GRADUATION

Graduation..... what does that mean
Arrived..... a new season..... a new chapter in life
A stepping stone upon life's path
A future to you..... as yet unknown.

With God's hand in yours
Ask Him to lead you along
Seek Him first in all you do
Find Him ever truthful and faithful to you
Opening doors, building bridges, restoring, healing
and renewing
Knowing.....
He is always there with you.

Hide His word in your heart
Evermore..... it will not depart
Invest yourself in His word
God will invest Himself in you.

Listen for God's voice..... and His call upon your life
Submit, yield, surrender your all
Stay hooked to The Vine
Mindful that wisdom and knowledge
It all comes from Him

Be filled with the Holy Spirit
Let Him teach you and guide you in The Way
Receive God's love..... be filled with His love
Abundant life is yours today.

In all your ways **acknowledge Him**
Lean not to your own understanding
Listening, hearing, yielding, trusting and obeying
Casting all your care upon Him.

Stay alert..... strong in faith believing
Knowing a battle is raging for your soul

Never give up or give in to despair
Defeat the enemy through Jesus name and His Word
And through prayer
And receive help and instruction from Him.

God is in control
Believe Him and find
Each new season . . . . . a great reason
To **trust** Him anew . . . . . all life through.

Remember . . . . . you are God's idea
Planned for before He made the heaven and earth
He will never abandon you or leave you alone
He is your Heavenly Father
Lovingly purchased by His precious Son
YOU belong to Him.

May God bless you and keep you
Causing His face to shine upon you
Making you aware of His Presence and power
Giving you eyes to **see** . . . . . ears to **hear**
And a heart to *know* Him.

May abundant love, joy and peace fill you and flow
through you
May you feel His great pleasure upon you
Now that is called . . . . . success!

Upward and onward dear graduate
God's plans for you are good
Enjoy life to the fullest
Know by Him . . . . .
You are Oh so loved and understood!

GIVING

A gift of affirmation
Lifts the spirit
Hugs the heart
Gives encouragement
Straight from the Father's heart.

What have we received this day?
What can we share with others, too?
Someone needs to hear a kind word
It can come through me and you.

Gifts received and given out
Comforting a soul to be restored
Multiplies the joy
And we will receive more.

A smile, a hello and looking another in the eye
Says I see you . . . . . you matter
People hunger for an affirmation such as this
We can share our joy hoping they will receive this.

God is the source of all comfort
and encouragement, you see
We are His earthly hands and feet
Given the privilege of distributing this
A building block in another's life
From God to you and me.

"Blessed be the God and Father of our Lord Jesus Christ, the Father of mercies and God of all comfort, Who comfort us in all our afflictions, so that we may be able to comfort those who are in any affliction with which we ourselves are comforted by God." 2 Corinthians 1:3,4 ESV

THAT GLORIOUS DAY

Glorious will be the day
When every knee shall bow
Every tongue confess
That Jesus Christ is Lord!

Such praise and worship due His name
The earth has never seen
Nor ear has ever heard
Even the rocks shall sing.

What an awe filled sight and sound
Every tongue from ever nation shall be spoken
With arms raised in praise before Him
Confessing and singing holy, holy, holy is our Lord.

If we on earth could hear the heavenly angels rejoicing now
With thanksgiving day and night as they praise Him so
We, too, could not help but enter in
Contagious joy . . . . . as our offering to Him.

God, you create the fruit of our lips
May we not be earthly hampered
May our hearts and lips be filled with praise
Joyously giving honor and glory to the King of Kings.

The glorious return of the Lord is coming
It could happen in a blinking of an eye
Let us encourage one another to present ourselves to God
Now . . . . . while there is still time.

Love, joy, purpose and peace will be found now
The Holy Spirit residing within
Made one with the Father and the Son
Forever settled . . . . . Soon we will be with Him!

*"Therefore God exalted Him to the highest place and gave Him the name
that is above every name, that at the name of Jesus every knee should
bow, in heaven and on earth and under the earth, and every tongue*

confess that Jesus Christ is Lord, to the glory of God the Father. " —
Philippians 2:9-11 NKJV

"Therefore, I urge you, brothers and sisters, in view of God's mercy, to offer your bodies as a living sacrifice, holy and pleasing to God—this is your true and proper worship." Romans 12:1 NKJV

A LOVE RELATIONSHIP

Relating to God as creature to Creator
Sheep to Shepherd
Subject to the King
Clay to the Potter
Child to the Father
I worship Him and thank Him
The King of Kings.

Leaning not on my own understanding
But in all my ways acknowledging God
I do not have to have all my life's answers at once
I relinquish my life..... trusting Him.

Trusting God to lead me
Hand in hand with me down my pathway of life
Intimately drawing me closer
Like a moth that is drawn to the light.

Encouraging and comforting, God says to me
Closer, my child, come closer
I have delivered you from the dark of night
Fear not any evil tidings
I have overcome them with My might.

Closer, My child, come closer
Lean hard..... lean harder still on Me
Forgetting what was past, pressing on
See..... I am doing a new thing.

Be like a tree planted by the rivers of living water
Sending out roots, drinking deeply from My source of life
Bringing strength and nourishment to your soul
To become as an oak tree of my righteousness
Tall, lofty and magnificent
Upright in My sight.

Limitless, unconditional love for you
No performance needed to make it your own
No working out your salvation with angst
My love to make you whole
Set free to be all you need to be.

How it grieves Me to see My children
Trying harder and harder, yet never achieve
The feeling of "good enough to be loved"
Not believing I AM says it is enough..... not your works
But..... just trusting Me
Nothing in your hands you bring to gain acceptance
Not striving..... just receiving My love.

I have led you down path's of righteousness for My
name's sake
Finding fulfillment through living close to Me
A path maybe not always of your choosing
But it is My way for you to be.

Sometimes hard, slippery places it is true
Heartache and loss a part of it too
Independence being broken
Emptiness..... dissatisfaction showing through
All meant to bring you so much closer
Transformed..... with a heart renewed.

Not designed to figure out the future
Engaged in excessive planning..... a need to control
But so we could have union and communion
You, My love, designed to be a part of Me..... I love you so.

Each day, each moment comes with a choice
What will I believe as truth?
Whom or what will I seek after?
A might battle rages on day and night.

Heaven and earth intersects the mind
Help me, God, establish Your way

Show me Your perspective
Continually, breath by breath
My desire..... only to please you
Your desire..... to bring it to pass.

Eternal life..... living forever
Waiting to call home His bride
Peace, not as the world gives
Rest, refreshed, renewed
In My presence..... fulness of joy
Love and acceptance
Plans for your good
Reality..... not just implied.

FREED TO BE ME..... AND SOARING

Things in my heart
Like a locked chamber
Beyond written..... hidden
Waiting to awaken and be expressed.

Like a bird..... cramped in a cage
With such a longing in its heart
Desiring to be set free.

When that day finally comes
The door opens up wide..... I can fly
Free..... at last..... set free.

Streaming across the open sky
"Unfettered..... unfettered is my cry"
I can fly uninhibited like never before
With joy I fly on as a bird on the wing
Unlimited space to soar..... to soar..... and to soar.

Deep unto deep is calling
For a safe place prepared for me
To be free from strife
In the ocean of life
I will stop..... I will look..... and I will see.

A Stone, The Chief Cornerstone
Jesus..... providing a home that is firm
Built on an unshakeable foundation
Purchased by His precious blood alone.

I am safe now
My heart can rest now
My spirit is set free now
To express what has been invested in me
I soar..... and soar..... and soar
Alive like never before.

CPSIA information can be obtained at www.ICGtesting.com
Printed in the USA
BVOW03s0325170415

396518BV00006B/10/P